Fun Adventure Crafts

Pirate Ship Adventure Crafts

Anna Llimós

Enslow Elementary
an imprint of
Enslow Publishers, Inc.
40 Industrial Road
Box 398
Berkeley Heights, NJ 07922
USA

http://www.enslow.com

Con

tents

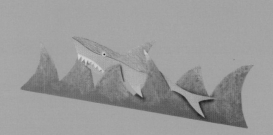

"A-ha! A ship!"

I have spotted an enemy ship!

Materials

- clay
- rolling pin (Ask permission first!)
- toothpicks
- scissors

1. Mix different colors of clay. Make a little mound of clay. Stick a toothpick in it.

Parrot

3. Stick the parrot's body on top of the toothpick in the mound.

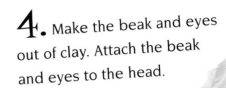

4. Make the beak and eyes out of clay. Attach the beak and eyes to the head.

2. Make the parrot's body from clay. Use a toothpick to decorate the tail. Make a ball for the head. Attach it to the body with a toothpick.

5. Flatten out a strip of clay. Cut out a rectangle to make two wings. Use a toothpick to decorate the wings. Place the wings onto the parrot's back. Bend them a little.

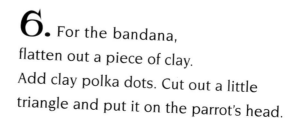

6. For the bandana, flatten out a piece of clay. Add clay polka dots. Cut out a little triangle and put it on the parrot's head.

1. Mold a thick, short piece of clay for the top half of the body. Mold another thick, longer piece of clay. Use the plastic knife to split it down the middle to make the legs. Attach the body to the legs with a toothpick.

Materials

* clay
* plastic knife
* dowel
* rolling pin (Ask permission first!)
* toothpicks

2. Make a boot out of clay. Attach it to the leg with a toothpick. Stick the dowel into the other leg. Make the belt and attach it to the waist.

3. For the arms, use two long pieces of clay, any color you wish. Attach a hand at the end of each arm. Use the rolling pin to flatten out a piece of clay. Cut a trapezoid from the flattened clay. Wrap it around the body. This will be the coat.

4. Attach the arms with toothpicks, one on each side of the body. A ball of clay will be the head. Use clay to make an eye and an eye patch. Attach the eye and the patch to the head. Attach the head to the body with a toothpick.

Enemy off the starboard side!

Captain Redbeard

Yarrrgh!

5. Roll out long, thin strips of clay for the hair. Use the rolling pin to flatten out a piece of clay and cut out the beard. Use a toothpick to decorate the beard and attach it to the face. Stick a nose on top of the beard.

6. Form a hat out of clay and put it on the pirate's head.

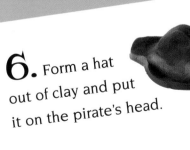

Pirate Girl and Crew

Materials

- clay
- card stock
- yarn
- crepe paper
- marker
- colored pencils
- white glue
- scissors

3. Decorate the pants with colored pencils. Draw stripes or any other design you wish. Glue the pants and T-shirt to the pirate girl's body. Let dry.

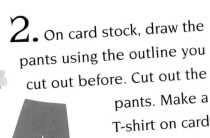

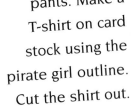

1. On card stock, draw the outline of a pirate girl and cut it out.

2. On card stock, draw the pants using the outline you cut out before. Cut out the pants. Make a T-shirt on card stock using the pirate girl outline. Cut the shirt out.

4. Cut out a rectangular piece of crepe paper. Glue it to the waist like a sash. Draw a sword on card stock and cut it out. Make a little cut in the sword's handle so it can be held in the girl's hand.

5. Draw the face with colored pencils, drawing a patch on one eye. For her hair, tie pieces of yarn into two bunches and glue it to the head. Let dry. Stick the finished figure into a piece of clay to make her stand.

6. Follow the same steps to make the rest of the crew. Make as many pirates as you wish. Decorate them as you wish.

Aargh!

What sailors!

Materials

- clay
- thick cardboard
- craft sticks
- poster paint
- card stock
- paintbrush
- white glue
- scissors

1. Make the shape of a cannon out of clay. On the narrow end, make a little opening.

Cannon

The pirates fire!

7. Glue the four wheels to the cart. Let dry. Put the cannon on it and stick the cloud of smoke in its opening.

2. Make four balls and four thin strips of clay. Wrap the strips around the cannon. Put one of the four balls of clay on the end of the cannon. The other three will be the cannon balls.

3. Draw a cloud of smoke on card stock. Cut it out. Paint it to look like smoke and fire.

4. Use thick cardboard to make the cart the cannon will be put on.

Fire!

5. Glue the cardboard together. Let dry. Cut out four wheels from the cardboard.

6. Ask an adult to help you cut the craft sticks to the right size. Glue them to the cardboard. Let dry.

11

Pirate Ship

Materials

* corrugated paper
* small cereal box
* card stock
* white glue
* colored pencils
* crayons
* stapler
* scissors

1. Draw the outline of the side of the ship on corrugated paper. Cut it out.

2. Using the first outline as a template, draw and cut out the other side.

6. Glue a piece of corrugated paper onto the top part of a small cereal box. Let dry.

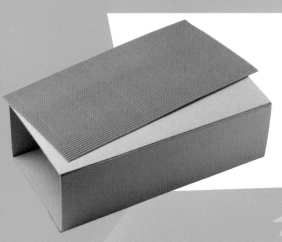

5. Glue the rails onto the same side you have the windows. Let dry.

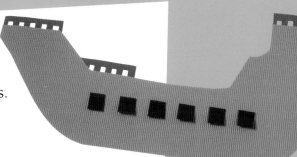

4. Cut out rails of different lengths from corrugated paper.

3. For the windows, cut six small squares out of corrugated paper. Glue them to one of the sides of the ship. Let dry.

7. Glue the two sides of the ship to both sides of the box. Let dry.

Long live Redbeard!

8. For the plank, cut out a strip of corrugated paper. Fold it and glue it to the side of the ship. Let dry.

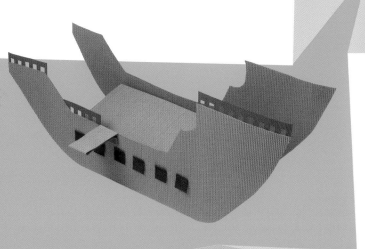

9. For the ship bow, cut out a triangle and staple it, bringing together the two front parts of the ship.

10. Draw a mermaid on card stock. Cut her out. Glue her to the bow of the ship as a figurehead. Let dry.

11. Draw some waves on card stock. Cut them out and decorate them with crayons. Glue them to the sides of the ship. Let dry.

Mast

Materials

- clay
- dowel
- wooden skewers
- card stock
- felt
- cloth
- white glue
- poster paint
- string
- paintbrush
- scissors

5. For an open sail, cut out a square piece of cloth and knot a piece of string at each corner. Tie the corners to the two skewers.

4. For a rolled up sail, tie a piece of white cloth to a skewer with string.

3. For the railing, fold the rectangles upward. Glue a strip of card stock around the top. Put it on the mast.

1. Make a ball out of clay and flatten it out. Stick the dowel into it. Wrap a strip of clay around the bottom part.

2. To make the crow's nest, draw a circle on a piece of card stock with rectangles around it. Cut it out and make a hole in the center.

6. Tie the rolled up sail above the crow's nest with string. Tie the open sail below the crow's nest.

The mast is ready!

7. Cut out a rectangle piece from felt. Paint a skull and crossbones or any other symbol you want on it. Let dry. Cut some fringe on one side. Glue the other side around the mast. Let dry.

Cabin Boy

Materials

* clay
* craft wire
* felt
* toothpick
* white glue
* scissors
* rolling pin
  (Ask permission first!)
* marker

The cabin boy fixes the flag!

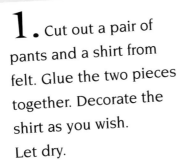

1. Cut out a pair of pants and a shirt from felt. Glue the two pieces together. Decorate the shirt as you wish. Let dry.

2. On another piece of felt, trace the outline of the shirt and pants. Cut it out. Stick a twisted piece of wire in between the two sets of clothes. Glue them together. Let dry.

6. Stick the head on the end of the wire that comes out of the top of the body.

5. Make the head out of clay. Use clay to make a nose, eyes, and ears. Attach them to the head. Draw a smile with the toothpick.

7. To make a bandana, use the rolling pin to flatten out a ball of clay. Add clay polka dots. Cut out a triangle and wrap it around the cabin boy's head.

Oof!
Done!

4. Make the feet and hands out of clay. Stick them on the ends of the wires that come out of the arms and legs.

3. For the arms, cut out a long, thin rectangle from felt. Glue a piece of wire to the middle. Let dry. Fold the felt in the middle. Glue the arms to the body behind the shirt. Let dry.

1.
Fold a rectangle of card stock in half. Draw some waves on one side and cut them out.

Materials

+ card stock
+ colored pencils
+ crayons
+ white glue
+ scissors

2. Color the waves with crayons.

4. Decorate the shark's back with colored pencils.

3. Draw a shark on card stock and cut it out.

Shark

The shark is hungry!

5. To make an eye, cut out a circle from card stock and draw in the pupil with a colored pencil. Glue it to the shark's face. Let dry.

6. Draw some teeth on card stock. Cut them out and glue them into the shark's mouth. Let dry. Put the shark in the waves.

Prisoner

Materials

- clay
- string
- toothpicks
- plastic knife
- rolling pin
  (Ask permission first!)
- scissors

5. Stick a toothpick into each leg. Make the feet out of clay and put them on the legs.

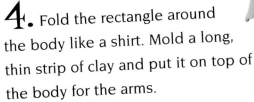

4. Fold the rectangle around the body like a shirt. Mold a long, thin strip of clay and put it on top of the body for the arms.

1. To make the legs, take a thick, long piece of clay and split it down the middle with the plastic knife.

3. Flatten out a piece of clay with a rolling pin. Cut out a rectangle.

2. Bend the legs and make pant cuffs with two strips of clay.

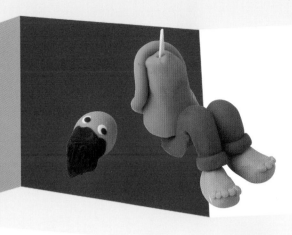

6. Make a ball of clay for the head. Make eyes and a little flat piece of clay for the beard. Decorate the beard using the toothpick. Attach the eyes and beard to the head. Attach the head to the body with a toothpick.

7. Make the hair out of thin strips of clay. Mold the nose. Attach the hair and nose to the head. Tie some string around the prisoner's body.

The shipwrecked sailor is taken prisoner!

A treasure map!

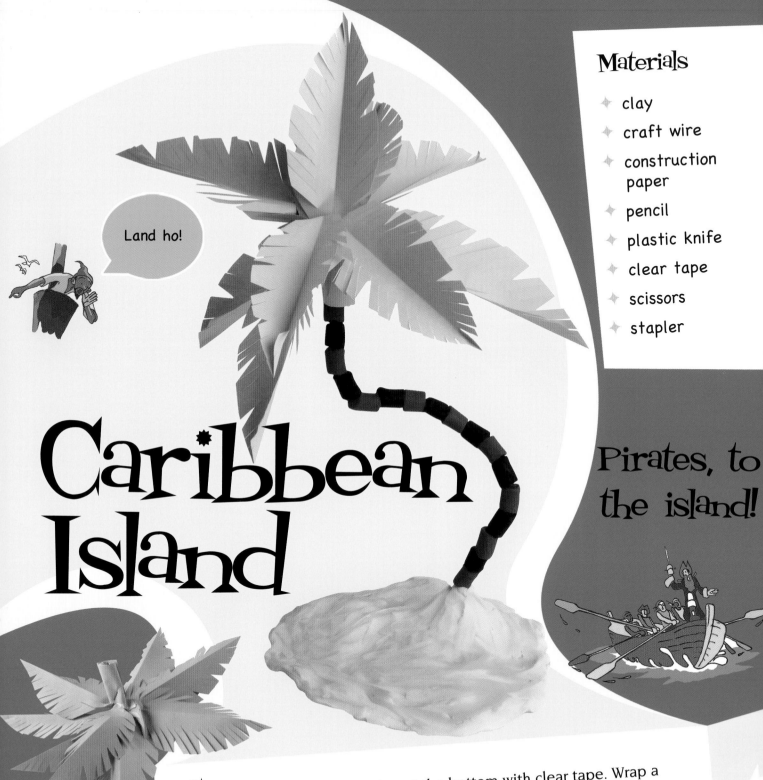

Land ho!

Caribbean Island

Materials

- clay
- craft wire
- construction paper
- pencil
- plastic knife
- clear tape
- scissors
- stapler

Pirates, to the island!

6. Join all the leaves together at the bottom with clear tape. Wrap a piece of construction paper around them to make a little tube and staple it together. Put the leaves on top of the trunk by sticking the end of the wire into the tube of paper.

1. For the sandy beach, mix different colors of clay. Make a mound out of clay. Stick a piece of wire in the middle of it.

2. Roll two long, thin pieces of clay. Cut them into pieces with the plastic knife.

3. Push the pieces of clay down the wire. This is the trunk of the palm tree.

5. Fringe the side of the leaf and unfold the paper. Make more leaves of different sizes.

4. To make the leaves of the palm tree, fold a piece of construction paper in half. Draw half a leaf and cut it out with the paper still folded.

Treasure Chest

Materials

- clay
- poster paint
- colored beads
- fishing line
- card stock
- plastic knife
- rolling pin (Ask permission first!)
- flat toothpicks
- white glue
- scissors

4. For the top of the chest, glue on more toothpicks to join the two half circles. Let dry.

3. Paint some flat toothpicks. Let dry. Glue them to the sides to form the walls of the chest. Let dry.

1. Make a flat strip of clay with the rolling pin. Cut the rectangular base (the long side should be the length of a toothpick) and the sides of the chest. Cut the sides of the top into half circles.

2. Glue the sides to the base. Let dry.

5. Place the top on the chest. Put two toothpicks at the front to hold it half open.

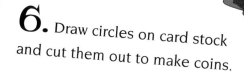

6. Draw circles on card stock and cut them out to make coins.

7. Make bead necklaces and put them into the chest along with the coins.

Treasure for the captain!

Create your own story with all the crafts in this book!

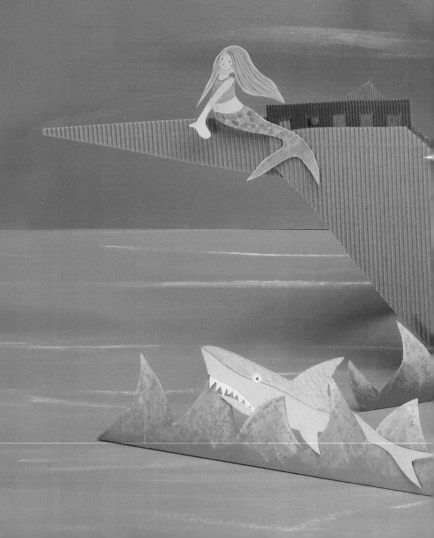

Somewhere at sea...

A chatty parrot, the pirates' pet, suddenly spies a ship on the horizon.

The great Redbeard shouts, "Battle stations!"

The pirate girl and her crew are resting when Redbeard shouts, "All hands on deck!"

The cannons on Redbeard's ship fire at the enemy.

In the end, Redbeard hits his enemy. The crew leaves the sinking ship, firing off one last cannonball.

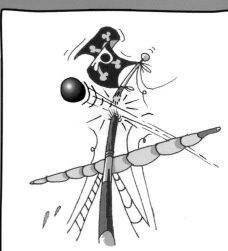

The flag is hit by the enemy's last cannonball.

The cabin boy, who is cleaning the deck, has to replace the flag. He sees a shipwrecked sailor from the sunken ship.

There are sharks in the water! One of the sharks has spotted the shipwrecked sailor!

Redbeard's crew rescues him and takes him prisoner.

The prisoner has a treasure map!

They sail to the island. Once the island has been sighted, they row to land in a boat.

They read the map and dig a hole where X marks the spot. They find a treasure chest full of jewels, coins, and gems!

Until the next pirate adventure!

Enslow Elementary, an imprint of Enslow Publishers, Inc.
Enslow Elementary® is a registered trademark of Enslow Publishers, Inc.

English edition copyright © 2011 by Enslow Publishers, Inc.

Translated from the Spanish edition by Stacey Juana Pontoriero.
Edited and produced by Enslow Publishers, Inc.

Library-in-Cataloging Publication Data

Llimós Plomer, Anna.
[Crea tu. Barco pirata. English]
Pirate ship adventure crafts / Anna Llimós.
p. cm. — (Fun adventure crafts)
Includes bibliographical references and index.
Summary: "Provides step-by-step instructions on how to make eleven
simple pirate-themed crafts, such as a ship, pirate crew, treasure chest,
and more, and it includes a story for kids to tell with their crafts"—
Provided by publisher.
ISBN 978-0-7660-3728-1
1. Pirates—Juvenile literature. 2. Handicraft—Juvenile literature. I.
Title. II. Title: Barco pirata.
G535.L61513 2010
745.5—dc22
                        2009041461
ISBN-13: 978-0-7660-3729-8 (paperback ed.)

Originally published in Spanish under the title *Crea tu . . . Barco
pirata*.
Copyright © 2008 PARRAMÓN EDICIONES, S.A., - World Rights.
Published by Parramón Ediciones, S.A., Barcelona, Spain.

Text and exercises: Anna Llimós
Illustrator: Àlex Sagarra
Photographs: Nos & Soto

Printed in Spain

122009 Gráficas 94 S.L., Barcelona, Spain

10 9 8 7 6 5 4 3 2 1

To Our Readers: We have done our best to make sure all
Internet Addresses in this book were active and appropriate
when we went to press. However, the author and the publishers have no control over and assume no liability for the
material available on those Internet sites or on other Web
sites they may link to. Any comments or suggestions can be
sent by e-mail to comments@enslow.com or to the address
on the back cover.

Read About

● *Books*

j 745.594 3/27/15 OCLC

Rees, Lesley. *How to Be A Pirate in 7
Days or Less.* Boston: Kingfisher, 2006.

Sadler, Judy Ann. *The New Jumbo Book of
Easy Crafts.* Toronto: Kids Can Press,
2009.

● *Internet Addresses*

Pirates! National Geographic
<http://www.nationalgeographic.com/
pirates/>

Pirate Crafts, DLTK's Crafts for Kids
<http://www.dltk-kids.com/crafts/
pirates/pirates.html>

Index